No 40-Year Journey

ISBN: 978-1-7350143-5-7

Library of Congress: 2020911289

Copyright © Steven Kenan

Publisher and Editor: Fiery Beacon Publishing House, LLC

Fiery Beacon Consulting and Publishing Group

This work was produced in Greensboro, North Carolina, United States of America.

No

40 Year

Journey

By

Steven T. Kenan

Table of Contents

Acknowledgements

Introduction

Acknowledgments

I thank God for giving me the wisdom and knowledge to

write this book to the world.

My wife, Tamara, and son, Israel have inspired me day by day to continue on the road to push the pen. Their love and support keep me striving for greater heights and deeper depths of seeking the glorified God for our household.

I would also like to give thanks to my Chosen Generation Family for the many prayers and support during this time of my life. You guys are absolutely amazing! CG4life - Big things popping and little things dropping!

To every reader, thank you for going with me on this journey. Together as heirs of Christ we shall win and will not go on a forty-year journey. My heart is filled with love and my eyes are flooded with tears as I say thank you.

To God be all the glory for what happens now and later in my life! Help me to die to my flesh that Your spirit may work through me. Amen.

Introduction

Let me start first by giving honor to the Almighty God for giving me the ability to write this book. I am grateful and thankful to every reader. As you read this book, I pray that it inspires you on your journey of life to continue to break down strongholds in your life and most of all, put God first in your life's journey. I pray that this book finds itself in the hands of men and women that have not confessed Christ as Savior and Lord. While I am still a work in progress, my life is a testimony of the struggle with guilt, hurt, shame and defeat and how I grew, got on the path of fulfilling God's purpose in my life and became equipped to conquer every battle in life by putting God first.

Chapter 1
How Did I Get Here?

Have you ever been on this journey called life and thought to yourself, "How did I get here," only to realize that "where" is absolutely nowhere? "Where" quickly becomes "

not where I thought I should be, where I wanted to be, what I hoped to be, what I dreamed to be and not where I said I would be." So how did I end up here? See, on my journey called life I found myself on what I call, a 40-year journey.

The question may be asked, what is a 40-year journey?

"For the children of Israel walked forty years in the wilderness, till all the people *that were* men of war, which came out of Egypt, were consumed, because they obeyed not the voice of the LORD: unto whom the LORD swear that he would not shew them the land, which the LORD swear unto their fathers that he would give us, a land that flows with milk and honey."

Joshua 5:6 KJV

God does not want us to be like the children of Israel wandering around on a forty-year journey. Studies show that the journey should have only been eleven days, but because of disobedience and complaining they went on a forty-year journey and never entered into the promise land. God has a land for us flowing with milk and honey with many promises, blessings, and miracles. I was like the people of Israel. On my journey at one time, I caused the journey to be prolonged because of disobedience which caused me to travel without a purpose, without a plan and no direction.

As I walk through this journey called life, I found out that there were a few things that was hindering me along the way; one of those things was that I was not seeking God first.   Without knowing that I was truly on a forty-year journey, I began asking myself," How did I get here?"

"But seek ye first the kingdom of God, and his righteousness; And all these things shall be added unto you." That's not what I was doing on my journey."

I was not a seeker of the kingdom. I was a seeker of God's hands but not His way. What is God's way -

simply His way of doing things which is His will for our lives. Yes, I was born again believer, but it had not been taught in the fullness of how to properly seek the Kingdom. I am a firm believer that whenever we as believers do not seek the Kingdom, it will cause us to make decisions fully off of our emotions and fleshy desires that God never ordained for our lives. This causes us to go on a 40-year journey. We find ourselves spending many invaluable years in relationships, friendships, on jobs and in churches feeling stuck without enough, a constant void feeling incomplete and most of all with the lingering question, "How did I get here?" What I had to come to understand was that being saved was awesome, but it was not enough. I needed a personal relationship with God. We all need a personal relationship with God so that on this journey of life we can see the hand of God move on our behalf.

We as believers, sons and daughters of the Most-High God, if we begin to seek His kingdom and all of His righteousness, God will begin to add all things to our life. Whenever you seek the Kingdom through prayer, worship, fasting and praise, God will begin to open up the treasures and mysteries in your life one day at a time; this makes the journey worthwhile, but you have to seek Him. At one point in my life I was not seeking God and His kingdom; I was making decisions without seeking God. I moved to another city without seeking God. I was getting in relationships without seeking God. I was getting into friendships without seeking God and even going to different churches without seeking God. One may have the question, "Is it really that serious to seek God concerning all of these things?", and my answer is YES!

Wrong people or things at the right time can cause things that was never ordained for your life to happen. What do I mean by right time and wrong things? When everything is going well and in order, all of a sudden Satan may send something that is not ordained of God and it throws everything off balance. If I am not seeking God and His plan for my life, then I will not see that the house, car, job, relationships and etc., as a wrong thing sent in my life to throw me off the plan. I was in the right timing, but I allowed a wrong thing to infiltrate my journey. Not seeking God on my journey was a big hindrance. This was causing me to go on a 40-year journey.

On your journey you must know who is sitting at your table. At the last supper Jesus had a table prepared and had twelve disciples at His table. He knew them all spiritually and naturally; He even knew which one was going to betray Him and He knew which one was going to deny Him. I ask a question: Do you know who is sitting at your table on your journey? When we fail to know who is sitting at our table, we will continue to have right time and wrong people as well as wrong things. This makes us constantly miss our destination. Doing things on your journey without seeking God can cause all kinds of mixed emotions to rage on the inside of you, which causes your journey to become stagnated to a point where you break down.

For I know the plans I have for you, Saith The Lord. They're plans for good and not for disaster, to give you a future and a hope.

Jeremiah 29:11 NLT

What I did not realize was that God had a plan for my life, but I had my own plan. As long as I was on my own plan and not seeking God's kingdom first, it was causing me to actively move within my 40-year journey. I was shouting, dancing and praising God for my idea of what I wanted to do in my life but I did not realize that my idea did not match the heart of God's plan for my life. What we have to understand is that doing things our way and not the way God planned for us can cause damage on the journey. Going our own way leads to frustration, hurt, pain, bitterness, and giving up. We must get rid of our ideas of how we think our journey should be and get on God's plan. Remember the scripture was written, that God knows the plans for you. Never once did God say He had an idea for our life! God does not operate in ideas for our life but a plan. As long as I operate on ideas, I will always have the question, "How did I get here?"

Now I am at the place of exhaustion, no way out and every road that I take there is a block. How do I escape? I am trying to move forward but there is a blockage on every side. Frustration is setting in, more anger and more bitterness. I keep trying things my way but find out on my journey that I am just going in a revolving circle over and over again, year after year, month after month, week after week, day after day, hour after hour, minute after minute and second after second. Again, "How did I get here?"

Conclusion

No matter how difficult it may seem or how difficult It may get on the journey stay obedient to the voice of God. He knows all and He knows the best way for your life.

Prayer

Father God in the name of Jesus, give me the spirit of obedience to go through this life's journey. Even through difficult times help me to submit to your will in Jesus name

Amen!

Chapter 2
All Talk, No Game

Have you ever been ecstatic about a dream or vision or something that God has showed you concerning your life? You were so optimistic that you had to tell your family and friends and even went as far as to write it all down? As the word of God declares:

"And the Lord answered me, and said, Write the vision, And make it plain upon the tables, that he may run that readeth it."

Habakkuk 2:2

I was writing the vision and making it plain; the problem was that I was not running with my own vision. I had all talk and no game. I could see things, I could even feel things and knew that God had greater for my life, but it seemed like I could never get in the game. There were times in life I could hear God calling me as he did Peter, but yet I continued on my own path of destruction!

"Do not be afraid. **"Peter spoke** up and **said**, "Lord, if it is you, tell me to come out on to the water." **Jesus replied**, "Come." **Peter stepped out of the boat** and began to walk on the water.

As he took a few more **steps**, he took his eyes **off** of **Christ**, noticing the wind and rough waters."

Matthew 14: 28-29

That was me - I would always step off the boat but somehow found myself taking my eyes off God while allowing things that had no value to it distract me and finding myself stepping back on the boat. We must understand that God is calling us to step in places that are unfamiliar to us. The unfamiliar place are those places that are unknown and very uncomfortable. Sometimes that can be fearful because we as humans like to know where we are going and what it is going to be like when we get there. When we do not have that control, it can cause fear to set in and that was me; I was fearful of the unfamiliar or the unknown places that God wanted to take me.

At that time, I could not tell you why fear had such a grip on me. It was stopping me from stepping out and doing the things in life I knew God wanted me to do. I could hear God saying, **"If you step out, I will hold your hand like I did Peter! I won't let you drown!"** I always heard people say, "never question God," but I had so many unanswered questions. I remember asking God, "Okay if I step out in faith what am I stepping out on?" I could clearly hear a soft, still voice of love saying, **"Son you have my word to step out on and that's all you need."**

"So shall my word be that goeth forth out of my mouth: it shall not return unto me void, but it shall accomplish that which I please, and it shall prosper in the thing whereto I sent it."

Isaiah 55:11 KJV

God is letting us know in this passage of scripture that His word is His bond, meaning that God will always do what He promised to do. You can believe God when He says, "I will help you. **My word** is **my bond**." God was prompting me to step out on His Word and get back in the game!
Wow that sounds so amazing and easy, but fear was a lingering issue. I had all talk and no game.

Have you ever wanted to get in a nice pool and go for a swim, but you had to test the water with your toe or foot first? Even if someone told you the water was warm you still had to test it for yourself. That was me, always having to test things instead of trusting God's plan for my life. I would test the water from the boat, but if it felt uncomfortable or was not familiar to me, I would say, "oh no I'm not going in that water!" In other words I was telling God, "I'm not getting ready to move forward in life."

Sometimes in life we find ourselves dealing with what I call the F- Factor which is Fear vs Faith. Fear begins to speak louder than the words you have written, than the dreams you dreamed and the excitement that you had for life. If you are not careful, you will allow fear to outweigh the voice of God. How? You hear God say, "Come, come" but you hear fear say, "don't move." Fear begins to outweigh God's voice that is calling you to step out! Then fear loudly says, "What if you lose? What if you look crazy? What if you drown? You don't have all the resource that you need to step out the boat and you don't have the finances either!" You just sit there, wait and tell yourself, "I'm putting things in order. I will wait just a little while." Finally, you realize that years have gone by and you still do not have things in order! Fear has literally held you captive on your journey of life realizing that you are all talk and no game.

"For we walk by faith, not by sight."
2 Corinthians 5:7(KJV)

In order to stop "all talk and no game," we must know that fear for our life is never what God desired for us. Fear is from Satan and tries to stop us on our journey because he knows that we are predestined for greatness. We must understand that Satan has no power. The only thing that gives Satan power is feeding off the fear of humans. We must not walk in fear but Power!

God wants us to have the power we need to fight the devil off on our journey and love to spread throughout life to help others on their journey of life. He also wants us to have a sound mind, so when God bids us to come, we will be like a child, just as he or she hears the voice of their daddy calling them. The child moves instantly being well assured and with great confidence that daddy will protect by any means necessary. Likewise, we will be the same with our spiritual Daddy, moving instantly at His voice knowing with great assurance and confidence that God/Daddy has all power in His hands to see us through this life. We must remember not to walk by what we see but walk by faith in what we know and game time it will be!

"And we know that all things work together for good to them that love God, to them who are the called according to his purpose
When we began to know that all things work together for the good with great love for our God talk and game came began to walk together hand and hand and when two is walking together hand

and hand purpose will began to be fulfilled on our journey."

<u>Romans 8:28 (KJV)</u>

Conclusion

To the reader I implore you to dream again so that your vision will come to life by the move of God! Continue to put action behind your words and watch mountains move in your life.

Prayer

Father in the name of Jesus I pray now that I will dream big because I serve a big God that can do exceedingly and abundantly. Father help me to believe again in Jesus name

Amen

Chapter 3
Who's to Blame

When life does not go the way we planned, the easiest thing to do is blame someone or something for where we are in life; it is called the "blame game." Of course, it has to be someone else's fault for why my life is the way that it is. It is so easy to blame everyone for the downfalls on your journey. The reality for me was that I did not want to face the reality. Wow!!!

"For we are each responsible for our own conduct."
Galatians 6:5

In life, not being responsible for our own conduct can cause us to blame others. We have to take ownership of our actions and face our own demons so that deliverance can manifest in our life. I had to take ownership for all of my actions on my journey with an open mind and a ready heart to receive the truth. I had to ask myself questions such as, "Who told me to get in that relationship when I knew it wasn't going anywhere?" I thought at one point I could change people, and in the process, got hurt beyond measure. Instead of being responsible for my own conduct and decision, it was just easier to put the blame on my surroundings. I would say things like, "Why didn't anyone tell me about this? If they say they love me why wouldn't they have warned me."

I learned you have to love yourself so much, that you will never allow yourself to enter or remain in an unhealthy relationship. When you know something is not good, do not even waste your time. Love yourself and follow your instinct when involving yourself in a relationship. You have eyes to see - open them, so that you can see the enemy through what appears to be the glory of what you prayed or asked God for. You have ears to hear, so listen to the spirit; do not override what you hear.

You have been down this road far too many times. When we are wasting time on counterfeit blessings, things that appear to be real be revealed as fake. You have a mouth and tongue and it must be used properly to come against demons that tell you to stay in things that God has not ordained for you. Yes, it gets lonely on this journey, but at the end of the day you can do bad by yourself!

"Submit yourselves, then, to God. Resist the devil, and he will flee from you."

James 4:7 (NIV)

We must listen and face the truth outside of our desire, needs, wants and lust of the flesh. I had to learn that I can never change mankind and that God is the only one that can change people; even in that, they have to want if for themselves. We have to understand that every man has the liberty to change or remain the same. I have learned that if we do not follow this simple truth of life then really who is to blame?

It was hard for me to take the blame for many mistakes and even the things that were not my fault. I had to sit and think about my journey and the things that I blamed people for. The questions began to roll in my mind again: "Who told me to go to the party? Who told me to move here and there? Who told me join this church? Who told me join this and that in the church? Who told me to do something as simple as go to a dinner with the crowd? Who told me to go to the family reunion?" Truthfully, this list goes on and on. You can get so involved in the many things on your journey, go so many places and when trouble hits, we blame the person that invited us or the person who told us about "the opportunity." With anything that we involve ourselves in, we have liberty to get in it and liberty to get out of it. Again, who's to blame?

In all actuality, the blame was on me, but pride and stubbornness would not let me flip the mirror. Flipping the mirror can be a challenge but it is necessary for the journey. Flipping the mirror causes you only to see you and nobody else but you. It reminds me of the Disney cartoon Snow White when the wicked stepmother would talk to the mirror and ask questions. She was okay until the mirror told her the truth that she did not want to hear. The mirror will cause you to look at yourself eye to eye. The mirror will speak and one day reveal the truth and instead of you asking the mirror questions the mirror will turn and start asking you questions. The mirror will say, "Who told you to marry them? Who told you to have a child with them? Who told you to trust this or that? Who told you to move in with them?" You answer the mirror trying to put the blame somewhere. It talks back to you eye to eye and you see yourself broken blaming everyone for all the mess on your journey. One day the mirror speaks back to you and says, "You're to blame! Face it Sir! Face it Ma'am!" You did not ask God first. Everything that looks good and sound good is not always good.

"Be anxious for nothing, but in everything by prayer and supplication, with thanksgiving, let your requests be made known to God;"

Philippians 4:6 KJV

Yes, being anxious without prayer can cause a tornado on the journey. That is what Satan desires, to tear up everything on our journey.

John 10:10 warns us that the thief comes to steal, kill, and destroy, but promises that Jesus came for us to have life. The problem was that I could not have the full life He wanted for me until I faced the reality that I was to blame and took full ownership for my own life. I really did not do as the Word of God instructed me and that was "to be anxious for nothing but in everything pray." Yes, it is that serious; I was not praying about every move, relationship, church, invite, job, car, place of residence, etc. which allowed Satan to steal, kill, and destroy. You must pray, stop being anxious for the promise and begin believing according to *Philippians 1:6 NKJV* which states:

"Being confident of this very thing, that He who has begun a good work in you will complete *it* until the day of Jesus Christ."

With great confidence you and I can look into that mirror called the journey of life, face all truth, and stop the blame game knowing that we are to blame. We can get back on track knowing that our God will complete the great work in us once we are willing to take ownership of it.

Conclusion

To the reader lets always remember while on the journey of life to always examine oneself. Never be afraid to take ownership in your life for mistakes. The mirror is set humble yourself and accept what you see and make the change.

Prayer

Father in the name of Jesus help me not to blame others for my life. Help me to take ownership and face reality so that I may move forward with a pure heart in Jesus name.

Amen.

Chapter 4

My Mind Playing Tricks on Me

Your mind can be whatever you want it to be. Your mind can be good, or your mind can be evil. The mind can be your enemy or best friend; in my case my mind was my enemy. The mind has imagination, perception, thinking, judgement, language and memory. The mind becomes an enemy through an open gateway allowing Satan to enter. When Satan enters the mind, he brings all kinds of imaginations which are things that appear to be real but are actually false. When that gateway is open, it will change your language from positive to negative and your thoughts patterns from dreams to nightmares.

My mind became the enemy on my journey and began showing me all kinds of false imaginations. This made me to say, "I cannot do this! Man, it's too hard! I don't have enough time! I will put it off until tomorrow!" This place called "tomorrow" leads to years. You find yourself judging your journey before your really can get started. When you allow your mind to open that gateway of voices, wrong thoughts and imaginations, it leads to all kind of excuses such as, "I can't do it! That's just not for me."

You find yourself saying things like, "This just to justify not moving forward." The language begins to change because you become overwhelmed with imaginations, begin saying all kinds of negative things and find yourself stagnated because of the thought you let in your mind. Wow, my mind is playing tricks on me! Now you see more darkness on the journey than light. You need to be rescued out of the darkness, so you will not be lost on the way.   The mind has you captive telling yourself NO, NO, NO, NO, not realizing you cannot fight thoughts with thoughts. The mind is truly playing tricks on you because Satan knows that you are destined for greatness. He knows if he can have a battle in our mind, it will weigh us down until the the mind is tricked up with all kind of false imaginations and thoughts.

"Casting down imaginations, and every high thing that exalteth itself against the knowledge of God, and bringing into captivity every thought to the obedience of Christ;"
                                    2 Corinthians 10:5 (KJV)

I had to learn that my thoughts should never have me captive, but I needed to capture my thoughts as the Word of God instructed me to do. We must understand that the Word of God is like a treasure that is deep at the bottom of the ocean. The only way a treasure hunter finds the treasure that changes his life is by going deeper, and that is what I had to do, go deeper into the word of God. I had to go deeper because the word brings life in dead situations. In this life, we must consistently cast down imaginations - those false things that appear real and every high thing that exalt itself above God because every word out of the mouth of God brings life and life more abundantly.

We must close the gate and let Satan out for good. Even if he is on the outside of the gate yelling lies, we must continue to cast down everything that he throws at us bringing it into captivity. We must lock Satan's words up - he has no authority over us and all that ever comes out his mouth is lies. Who told you that you can't? Who told you that you are going to lose? Who told you that you would die? Who told you that you couldn't make it? Who told you that God didn't love you? Those are some of the many lies that Satan will tell us as we travel on our journey call life.

We must understand that we belong to our father who is big, strong and mighty and we will, by His grace and mercy, carry out the promises in this life. Why? Because We belong to God!

"Know that the Lord, he is God! It is he who made us, and we are his;[a] we are his people, and the sheep of his pasture."

Psalm 100:3 (ESV)

We must understand who has power over us and who does not have power over us. As Jesus said to Pilate:

"Then Pilate said to Him, "Are You not speaking to me? Do You not know that I have power to crucify You, and power to release You?" Jesus answered, "You could have no power at all against Me unless it had been given you from above."

John 19:10-11

Understanding that God has power over us and that Satan has no power over us unless giving from above should put our mind at ease on our journey. We do not belong to Satan, so everything he brings our way is a lie and we must trust and believe that our Father will protect us through our process.

"He was a murderer from the beginning, and abode not in the truth, because there is no truth in him. When he speaketh a lie, he speaketh of his own, for he is a liar and the father of it."

John 8:44

Satan was a murderer from the beginning of time and even from the beginning of our life he wanted to kill us. He wants to kill the promise and take us all off the journey or at least stop us. We must realize there is absolutely no truth in Satan for he is the father of lies. If we do not get a true understanding of the father of lies, Satan, our minds will play tricks on us.

Conclusion

To the reader, continue to allow God to renew your mind daily through prayer and cast down every thought that comes to your mind that tells you that you cannot succeed on your journey.

Prayer

Father in the name of Jesus I cast down every thought and imagination that exalt itself against the knowledge God. I bring my thoughts captive to your word and ask you to renew my mind daily Amen

Chapter 5

Laying Down

"Get up! Get up! Get up!" – this is what my mind was telling me, but I laid there. Where was I laying? I was laying in guilt, sorrow, disappointment, pain, laziness, excuses, lies and so much more. I did things my way for so long that it caused me to lay down on my journey. When you lay down, you find yourself going absolutely nowhere. You find yourself not really caring how you look anymore or where you are going. You find yourself just on the earth existing.

"Does it get that tough in life," and yes is the answer. I was so depressed that I did not care how I looked; the desire to look like something was not there because of going through so much. I am sure that at one point in your life you felt the same or are dealing with this now. The trials have overtaken you and the tribulations have weighed you down. The storm has consumed you and you stopped without knowing that you have literally laid down.

See laying down is just not a physical laying down on a bed or couch - laying down is doing absolutely nothing; no longer moving forward, no longer speaking to the mountains, commanding them to move, no longer dreaming, or trying to reach goals. You no longer have any goals. At this point, you find yourself putting your life in the hands of people wanting or needing them to do majority of everything for you because you have simply laid down.

The "get up" that you once had is completely gone. Oh yes, you are still working a job that you hate and doing things in life that are not producing any fruit; you are just moving without a purpose, moving without a plan, moving without a destiny. Why, do you ask? The answer is clear - because you have laid down without knowing.

All of this was me. I felt as though I had laid down in the bottom of a pit with no way out of the pit. I was in the wilderness and could not even cry out because of all the wrong turns, mistakes and wrong decisions. This pushed me to quit and lay down. I learned that you can work a job and not even realize that you quit. You can get up every morning and not realize that you quit. You can go to church and still not realize that you quit. You can even be in a marriage and not knowing that you quit. You could be raising your kids and not realize that you quit. You can be doing all kinds of things on your life journey without concluding that, "I really have quit."

The mindset tells you, "Oh well, at least I'm doing something, and something is better than nothing." That may be true, but I found out that type of mentality will rob you of your true happiness. I honestly believe that God wants us to be happy in this life despite all trials and tribulations we may face. God does not want us to have that "just enough to get by" mindset. When you have that mindset, you live life and miss out on so many opportunities, things like traveling to see the world, stepping out on faith to get that dream job or position, activated callings that you are called so much more. We could sit back and sing the song, "Long as I got King Jesus, I don't need nobody or nothing else," and trust that it is true. Jesus is all we need but we must also know that King Jesus want His people happy, blessed and the list goes on! Jesus did not just give his life for us just to be saved and be limited to that one act!

"For God so loved the world, that he gave his only begotten Son, that whosoever believeth in him should not perish, but have everlasting life."

John 3:16 (KJ)

Jesus has also given us benefits on this earth and God wants to load us up daily with those benefits while on this earth.

"Blessed be the Lord, who daily loadeth us with benefits, even the God of our salvation. Selah!"

Psalm 68:19

Jesus our Lord has given us Himself and also a never-ending package of benefits that we can receive daily, but you must get back up again. How do I get myself up from here? How do I move forward? How do I get back on the journey? How do I live again? How do I dream again? How do I hope again? The world itself has swallowed me, and I find myself laying down doing absolutely nothing.

"Jesus saith unto him, Rise, take up thy bed, and walk."

John 5:8 (KJV)

The word of God is the key to getting up. The first thing Jesus told the man to do was rise! That is the first thing I had to do - rise and listen to the command of Jesus. I had a choice to continue to lay there or rise and you have that same choice. Rising back up is the best feeling that we can ever encounter on our journey because now we get to dust ourselves off from laying so long! Clean yourself up from wobbling in the mess and clear your eyes up so you can see again! Clean out your ears so you can hear God voice clearly, and most of all, start back walking. Jesus told the man to take up his bed; if the man never took up his bed he would have never walked. The bed represents laying down, it represents someone waiting on you, it represents brokenness and being stagnate, and most of all, never having your own. I had to rise up and pick up my bed and walk and so do you. Rise up, pick up your issues, problems, excuses, lies, sorrows, lazy ways and walk. No longer do we have to lay down because destiny is calling our name.

Conclusion

Get up and live. Do not let your past cause you to lay in life. Let your past push you into your destiny because your past is producing your promise

Prayer

Father in the name of Jesus help me to walk by faith and not by sight. Give me the strength to rise up and take my place on my journey Amen.

Chapter 6

Lost but Now I'm Found

In this life we can become lost, but one of the greatest feelings is to be found especially when you are found by Jesus Christ and He finds you right where you are. I was found by Jesus Christ on my journey and I believe because I surrendered my will to the will of God, He found me.

When we surrender our heart, mind and ways to God, turn to Him and cry for help, then God can rescue us. Knowing that God will rescue us on our journey in times of trouble gives us back the confidence we need to get back on the journey. Wow, all this time I was causing myself to go in circles and all I had to do is surrender my will to the Father! This caused me to become fearless which caused Satan to lose power over me. Surrendering to God causes your troubles to go away and the light to shine again on your journey of life. It is like a breath of fresh air because your mind is transformed and even when the enemy tries to come up against you and try to get you off track You can rest safe and secure.

You are filled with hope and emptied of worry. I was lost but now I am found. The way of God will always lead you right. Now the rest that I needed on my journey is applied and I can continue in this life.

"Surrender your heart to God, turn to him in prayer, and give up your sins—even those you do in secret. Then you won't be ashamed; you will be confident and fearless. Your troubles will go away like water beneath a bridge, and your darkest night will be brighter than noon. You will rest safe and secure, filled with hope and emptied worry. You will sleep without fear and be greatly respected."

Job 11:13-19 (CEV)

In order to be found I had to get a mindset like Jesus when He was in the Garden of Gethsemane. Jesus was praying to the Father even on His journey just as we do today. Jesus wanted the cup to pass but it was not His will but God's. On our journey there are many things we will encounter that we would love to pass us by. It is a must that we take them on because I learned that it is necessary for our growth spiritually and naturally. My mother used to teach Sunday School Class when I was younger, and she had a saying that she would have us to say every Sunday before class:

"We are learning that we might live as we learn we are growing."

      Because of sayings like this I can honestly say I was lost but now I am found.

"saying, "Father, if it is Your will, take this cup away from Me; nevertheless, not My will, but Yours, be done."

Luke 22:42 (NKJV)

When we get a "nevertheless not my will but your will be done" mind, God will move outside of your understanding and blow your mind. Will the trials and tribulations stop coming? Of course not, but because you have turned your will over to the will of God, Jesus Christ will give you the strength you need to carry the cup that once seemed to heavy to bear.

      I was taught that in this life that I had to be strong in everything that I did but I found out that being strong or pretending to be strong sometimes can cause us to be lost along the way. At one point in my life, I thought that I had to prove to God that I was strong enough to handle every trial, strong enough to handle tribulations and strong enough to handle any storm that came up against me on my journey. This literally was causing me to be lost. It is so important on this journey that we study the Word of God and get a great understanding how Jesus Christ Himself walked this earth and how He made it through all trials, tribulations, persecution, storms and most of all, crucifixion.

I have some good news that will cause you to be found on your life journey – it is okay to be weak believe it or not! God rejoices when we are having weak moments in life because He wants us as His children to depend totally and completely on Him. The Bible tell us that Jesus Christ's strength is made perfect in our weakness. So, we must take a cup of Grace and Mercy every day and as many cups as we need to make it in this life. All we have to do is receive it by faith.

"And he said unto me, My grace is sufficient for thee: for my strength is made perfect in weakness. Most gladly therefore will I rather glory in my infirmities, that the power of Christ may rest upon me."

2 Corinthians 12:9

Now that is good news to know - that God's grace is sufficient for us in this journey of life. Sufficient, yes, meaning that it is more than enough and will never run out on us. On my journey, tapping into the true power of God's Grace and Mercy truly found me and gave me life on my journey. I always heard the song, "Amazing grace how sweet the sound," but to really understand Grace, sadly I did not. I remember when God revealed the message of grace to me through a woman of God who was a part of my ministry; I thought she was crazy as she explained it to me. At the moment, I began to judge something that I was not educated on. I asked her a question - "Are you saying we can sin and do whatever we want to do?" She told me, "Pastor ask the Holy Ghost to reveal it to you," and me being curious about grace, I began to pray and I ask God.

What I did not know was that I needed Grace on this journey. God began to reveal his grace to me through the gospel of Jesus Christ.

"And he said unto Jesus, Lord, remember me when thou comest into thy kingdom. And Jesus said unto him, Verily I say unto thee, Today shalt thou be with me in paradise."

Luke 23:42-43 (KJV)

When this was revealed to me, it found me even the more. This thief on the cross lived a reckless life but right at his end on the cross he had a request, and that was to be remembered when Jesus entered into the Kingdom. Jesus' answer to the thief blew my mind; the forgiveness, love and grace that was shown to this thief was unbelievable. It pierced my heart to know that the love of Jesus is the greatest love we can ever encounter in this life. God's grace through Jesus Christ gave the thief something that he did not deserve, prove or earn and that was Paradise with our Lord and Savior in the kingdom of heaven. The thief did not have to earn his way in or work his way in; all he had to do is believe. There are many more stories of grace that cause us to be found. I learned that I never had to prove myself to God and be so tough. Through His grace when we fall down His grace says, "get back up," and if we are lost His grace will find us. I was lost but now I am found. Many times I thought I had to start over from the beginning and I hated certain ways about myself that was causing me to be lost but now through the grace of the word of God I can rejoice in all my weakness knowing that I once was lost on this journey of life but now I am found.

"Because of the extravagance of those revelations, and so I wouldn't get a big head, I was given the gift of a handicap to keep me in constant touch with my

limitations. Satan's angel did his best to get me down; what he in fact did was push me to my knees. No danger then of walking around high and mighty! At first I didn't think of it as a gift, and begged God to remove it. Three times I did that, and then he told me, My grace is enough; it's all you need. My strength comes into its own in your weakness."

2 Corinthians 12:9-13 (MSG)

I was lost but now I am found. I was found by the Master Builder, found by the Creator! God Himself called me out of darkness and into His marvelous light. God will find us if we want to be found. There is a song that I love to sing that is called, "Lord it's in your hands." That is what I did on my journey, I placed everything in the Master's hands and because of that I am found. As the scripture said, Satan and his angels did their best to get me down but all it did was bring me down to my knees and establish a greater prayer life within me.

In this life, prayer is the key and will unlock some doors. Prayer became my best friend and a spiritual weapon against Satan and his angels. Prayer will most definitely keep you found but you have to be consistent with your prayer life because it is a form of communication to the Father. Jesus teaches us that we should pray all the time. This is not to worry us but to exercise us. Prayer will help us fight against impatience so that a long delay on our journey will not cause us to quit. I was lost, but now I am found.

Conclusion

I speak to your heart that you will continue to surrender to the will of God for your life and you will never be blind on your journey.

Prayer

Father in the name of Jesus, continue to renew my heart, take the scales off my eyes that I may see and understand your will for my life.

Amen

Chapter 7
My Word Is My Bond

Growing up, my mother would always tell me that actions speak louder than words. In order to have a successful journey you must have action behind every word that proceeds out your mouth. I remember one time while in prayer, I heard God say, "how bad do you want it?" Wow, what an awakening! I wanted what God had for me so bad that it was time to make my word my bond. One may say, "what do you mean when you say my word is my bond?" This phrase is used to indicate that one will always do what one has promised to do. I made a promise to myself this year - this will be the year that I finish my book by any means necessary. I had been talking about writing a book for many, many years. For many different reasons I kept putting it off. Action was needed - I had to make up in my mind and heart that this was the set time. I had to realize that procrastination was holding up the next move of God not only for my life but my family as well.

Procrastination is the action of delaying or postponing something. (Google dictionary) We must understand that we are like a treasure chest and on the inside, we are full of diamonds, but those diamonds will never be of any use or value if the treasure chest is kept closed. I decided to open up what God has put inside of me to change the world. Our words over our life can bring life or death and I decided to speak life. My word is my bond.

"Death and life are in the power of the tongue."
Proverbs 18:21 (KJV)

We must speak life on our journey. No matter what we feel, see or go through, our tongue is full of deadly poison. I learned that I had to love my life enough to speak life. As I began to travel on my journey there were several times that doors closed that was a disappointment but through spiritual growth, I learned that when one door closed God will open another. I learned to turn from that closed door that has been shut in my face and go to the next one.

To be in this journey and have action behind your words is life changing because you will begin to tell yourself, "I will no longer lie to myself and put things off." God's words are full of power and every word spoken out of His mouth is His bond. His word says:

"**So shall my word be that goeth forth out of my mouth: it shall not return unto me void, but it shall accomplish that which I please, and it shall prosper in the thing whereto I sent it.**"

Isaiah 55:11(KJV)

Now my word is my bond. In order for a farmer to get a harvest from the field he first has to plant the seeds. That is what I learned - to plant seeds over my life that I may reap a harvest full of promise and life.

Conclusion

Speak life and not death. Your words are powerful and can move mountains just by speaking. Remember, you have your Father's DNA. So, let's talk and make moves like our Father.

Prayer

Father in the name of Jesus I pray now that you allow my words to match my heart. My words are seeds in my garden of life, so I ask that you let me stay true to my word.

Amen

Chapter 8
Attitude Check

Traveling on this journey an attitude check is necessary because you will find out that several miracles that you will encounter require the right attitude to handle it. You need to be able to handle what you will see and what you will feel. We need to be able to handle how God will use us and pour out His many miracles in our lives. Understand that it is hard to fill a cup that is already filled; we must empty out so God can fill our cups as well as mind so we can experience the overflow!

At this point in my life, I had to have a moment to sit down as Jesus instructed His disciples at the Mount; He gave them their first assignment and that was to sit down and be taught. Jesus wants to teach and prepare us for what is coming on this journey and we cannot take the old attitude in new places.

Now when Jesus saw the crowds, he went up on a mountainside and sat down. His disciples came to him, he opened his mouth and taught them saying...
Matthew 5:1(NIV)

Jesus has to give us that attitude check on the way so that we can grow in this life but in order to get it, the first thing we need to do is sit down! It is important that you sit down so that you can stop being a tornado!

A tornado is a violent rotating column of air extending from a thunderstorm to the ground. (Google dictionary) The most violent tornadoes are capable of tremendous destruction with wind speeds of up to 300 mph. They can destroy large buildings, uproot trees and hurl vehicles hundreds of yards. On my journey, I had to sit down and get checked so I could stop destroying everything and everyone that I came in contact with. When your attitude changes about life, it is like the song:

"I can see clearly now that the rain is gone."

Have you ever been driving at night and a bad storm comes and prevents you from being able to see? You have your windshield wipers going as fast as they can go, but you still cannot see. The smartest thing to do is to pull over and sit until things calm down. When you sit and allow the storm to pass, God can speak while you wait in the storm. In this life, your attitude has to be checked in many areas. We have to check hatred, jealousy, envy, strife and more; it is called an attitude check! Our attitude is being checked to show us how to deal with different spirits, people, places and things.

He said: "Blessed are the poor in spirit, for theirs is the kingdom of heaven. Blessed are those who mourn, for they will be comforted. Blessed are the meek, for they will inherit the earth. Blessed are those who hunger and thirst for righteousness, for they will be filled. Blessed are the merciful, for they will be shown mercy. Blessed are the pure in heart, for they will see God. Blessed are the peacemakers, for they will be called children of God. Blessed are those who are persecuted because of righteousness, for theirs is the kingdom of heaven.

Matthew 5:3-12(NIV)

I have encountered many different trials and tribulations that could have caused many inside issues that would began to show up on the outside. In the Beatitudes, Jesus taught the disciples how blessed they were; He also taught them what to do when persecution came up against them.

The very thing that we all hate to run into is the very thing that makes us blessed and that is persecution. Being lied on and talked about, yes it hurts, but sit down and let Jesus teach you how blessed you are when this happens. Yes, you will want to get those people back who have done all of these things to you by any means necessary. We must remember what the Beatitudes say:

"Blessed are the peacemakers for they will be called the children of God."
Matthew 5:9

I learned that no matter what I go through on this journey, my peace will never be broken again, because my attitude has been checked. When you sit down as instructed and receive your attitude check, it will teach you how to love even your worst enemy and even how to bless them. We must have the right attitude every day. Satan tries to challenge us in this life and that is okay; just go sit down with God and have an attitude check. An attitude check it will help us ensure that we never have a dog who regurgitates his food and adopt a "go back and eat it later" mentality.

"As a dog returneth to his vomit: so a fool returneth to his folly."

Proverbs 26:11(KJV)

This passage of scripture was truly an attitude check for me because I did not want to be like that dog returning to the very thing God delivered me from. I had to refuse to be the fool that returned to his on folly, meaning someone who lacks the proper fear or respect for God - he or she is therefore prone to go in the wrong direction in life. One may say, "Is the attitude check necessary to endure on the journey," and I must say yes because it will set off the right energy that we will need to complete different assignments throughout life.

Jesus had the hardest journey and assignment that any man has ever encountered on this earth, but yet He endured. He endured being talk about, mistreated, lied on, persecuted, forsaken, betrayed, denied, beat all night, thorns placed on His head, standing in judgement, carrying the cross, was spat on, hit with rocks, nailed to a cross and pierced in His side. In all of this testing, He did not give up on His journey until the assignment was completed and HE said IT IS FINISHED according to John 19:30!

"When Jesus therefore had received the vinegar, he said, It is finished: and he bowed his head, and gave up the ghost."

John 19:28-30 (KJV)

We cannot stop any assignments on our journey until we are able to say the same words as Jesus, and that is, IT IS FINISHED! We must not conform to the world's way of doing and be transformed by the renewing of the mind by allowing God to help us.

So here's what I want you to do, God helping you: Take your everyday, ordinary life—your sleeping, eating, going-to-work, and walking-around life— and place it before God as an offering. Embracing what God does for you is the best thing you can do for him. Don't become so well-adjusted to your culture that you fit into it without even thinking. Instead, fix your attention on God. You'll be changed from the inside out. Readily recognize what he wants from you, and quickly respond to it. Unlike the culture around you, always dragging you down to its level of immaturity, God brings the best out of you, develops well-formed maturity in you.

Romans 12:1-2 The Message (MSG)

God is giving us an attitude check. It brings out the best in us and allow the worst things in us to die! The attitude check is a must on the journey because it causes us to die to our way of doing things. The great Apostle Paul stated, "I die daily." One may have a great concern with understanding that we must die daily. To clear that up, Paul basically is saying "deny yourself." I had to deny myself and I am still learning and striving to deny myself so that I can follow Jesus correctly. Deny yourself of pride, stubbornness and disobedience. This type of attitude check will cause us to be developed and mature to handle the things on our journey so we will not have a setback.

A new attitude on your journey is like new life that gives you a new view; it is like the blind man in the Bible who made the statement: "I once was blind but now I can see." What can you see? I see destiny over and over again! Nothing and no one will ever put scales over my eyes including myself again because of the new attitude. Everyone on your journey in this life must understand that destiny awaits you. In the natural when something gets in your eyes, it can drive you up the wall. A lot of it is accompanied by irritation, tearing, and even pain. While there could be a foreign particle on the surface of your eye, such as an eyelash or dust, you can experience this sensation even if there is nothing there. It can stop us from seeing clearly, and not to mention, it is beyond irritating. When we as humans have this type of experience with our eyes, our first thought is to let someone blow in our eyes or to wash our eyes out with eye wash because we want to see clearly. That is what I have learned on this journey - when my eyesight starts seeing things outside of my destiny, it is a must to wash my eyes out. You have to see this in the spirit. I wash my eyes out with the Word of God and believing and trusting in our God! Jesus made mud and put it in the blind man's eyes and told the blind man to go and wash in the pool of Siloam and he came back seeing. The blind man, I could only imagine, was filled with an unspeakable joy, full of hope and glory because his journey was dark and going nowhere but when he came in contact with Jesus all of that changed!

Certain men around him questioned his new attitude in his life and even asked, "Where did you get your sight from?" His response was, "Jesus." Even while being surrounded by many, being questioned and not believing, the blind man had to still believe.

And said unto him, Go, wash in the pool of Siloam, (which is by interpretation, Sent.) He went his way therefore, and washed, and came seeing.
The neighbours therefore, and they which before had seen him that he was blind, said, Is not this he that sat and begged? Some said, this is he: others said, He is like him: but he said, I am he. Therefore, said they unto him, How were thine eyes opened? He answered and said, A man that is called Jesus made clay, and anointed mine eyes, and said unto

me, Go to the pool of Siloam, and wash: and I went
and washed, and I received sight.

John 9:7-11 (KJV)

We must understand that sometimes this level of happiness and having this type of attitude will cause people that are around us to question what is going on. They may not even believe the change in your life, but like me, I am sticking to my story and that is:

I once was blind but now I see I have a new attitude and there's no stopping me now!

Let's keep our new attitude and eyes clear of danger on our journey and watch God carry us through!

Conclusion

Be ye transformed by the renewing of your mind. Get in God's presence and sit at His feet, so that you will be ready for what He has planned for you on your journey

Prayer

Father God in the name of Jesus, deliver me from my attitude and prepare me for your glory in my life. Father make me humble so I may learn your way and die to my way.

Amen

Chapter 9

Good Things Come to Those Who Wait

The waiting process can be a challenge, but good things come those who wait. In my journey, I desired to have a family. After going through so much drama with young ladies in relationships I finally came to the conclusion that "enough is enough." I believe when you get tired of being hurt or either hurting someone, it is just time to wait! Even as God began to prepare me for marriage, I had to be content with being single.

Not that I speak in respect of want: for I have learned, in whatsoever state I am, therewith to be content. I know both how to be abased, and I know how to abound: everywhere and in all things, I am instructed both to be full and to be hungry, both to abound and to suffer need. I can do all things through Christ which strengtheneth me.

Philippians 4:11-13 (KJV)

See what we must understand is that being single or married is not bad. When you are single, you must understand that it is just you and God and that time of freedom must be used wisely, because when the great day comes to be married, that changes to some degree. I found myself involved in relationships and being told that I "was not dating material, but I will look you up when I'm ready to be married," and dating someone that had a baby on me while going off to school! I even remember being told one night that the relationship may not work because of my skin completion and "I don't want dark kids." I knew that God had something special for me; it just would consist of me waiting. I remember plugging myself into my work, learning myself, and finding the new me that God was creating in preparation for me to become a husband. He would have me do some very strange things such as anointing the door. I would say, "the door God," and He would say, "Yes! You have to get in the spirit son and see yourself anointing her back."

I would leave notes on the refrigerator. When I went to church, I would touch the seat beside me and say, "one day" but I had to remember good things come to those that wait! One day I remember seeing a young lady that I knew of in a service but at that time I was okay with being by myself and I was enjoying life on my new journey. I found out God will send you exactly what you need in the wait when you take your mind off of it. After seeing the young lady that evening, I said to myself" hummm but nope!" I went to another service few weeks later and she was stunningly amazing, but I knew this young lady would not fall for me because, did I mention, we went to the same high school and I considered her one of the popular girls. I remember weeks went by and my Godmother at the time invited me to dinner. When I arrived there my Godmother informed me that her niece, the young lady that I had seen at the last two, services was coming. I wanted to get my plate and run but I stayed. We all sat down to eat dinner and as everyone began to fix their plates, I remember her saying to her aunt, "Are you going to fix your King's plate first?"

Immediately the hardness of "I'm not paying you any attention" or whatever the feeling was went down the drain. I was like Mary in the Bible when the angel of the Lord visited Mary and told her she was going to conceive a child which is the son of God and God said he shall be call Jesus the Savior of the world. Mary's response was, "How can this be I know not a man?" My response was very similar – "How can this be! I never meet a woman my age this mature; one who carries herself like a lady, with a voice and beautiful on the outside and inside." The next day this young lady and her aunt, which is my Godmother, came by my mother's house out of nowhere. Again, I was like Mary in the Bible – "How can this be," as I blushed. I wanted to run and go home because of the way I was dressed, but I knew deep down inside this lady was different compared to any woman I had ever encountered in my life. She was not a girl who needed the voice of friends and family but a woman that followed her heart and the voice of God. I will never forget - I took her for a ride that same day and took her back to my place just to show her where I lived. We walked in the apartment and when I told her that God instructed me to decorate my apartment like this for my wife, she smiled, but at the moment had little to say which puzzled me. I did not know at that time what to think. Did she smell something or was it something that she did not like? She told me at the end, "I love your apartment," but for me that just was not enough; something did not set well within me. I remember asking her, "You sure? Is something wrong?" She later told me that all the palm trees decorations were so amazing to see because her name, Tamara, meant palm tree. I echoed again, "yes God told me to decorate my apartment for my wife."

When I took her back, I remember we set with my mother and her aunt and in the conversation my Godmother stated that her niece could sing and then my mother responded saying, "My son can sing as well." (Yes, I was beyond embarrassed.) They proceeded to ask us to sing a song together and reluctantly both of us agreed. At that moment, something took place that neither one of us could explain. That night, we stayed on the phone all night until 6:00am the next morning and from that moment on we were inseparable.

Truly no games were being played; we both were very clear of what we wanted and needed, and it was so easy to share with each other. We began to go out and, not to mention, church together. We began to bond together praying and spending time together. This was so unreal but good things come to those that wait. Truly I believed and knew in my heart I had found my good thing as the Bible says.

He who finds a wife finds a good thing, And obtains favor from the Lord.
Proverbs 18:22 (NKJV)

We dated for a month and I proposed to her in church during a Sunday morning service. I later found out that was what God told her - that she would be proposed to in a church. Well, by the grace of God we got married the next day in my Pastor's home, the late Apostle Addie Collins! (Yes, I did say the next day.) My wait was truly over, and I had found my good thing.

Now both of us desired children but my wife had previously let me know that she could not have children. Immediately I touched her stomach and said you will birth a child. Four months in the marriage we found out that we were expecting and we were beyond happy for what God had done. Unfortunately, within a month, I remember receiving a call at work from my wife saying she lost the child. We both were devastated. We were hurt but we praised and trusted God together even in hurt believing that to lose is to gain. Within a month she was expecting again. Our hearts rejoiced at what God had done and God blessed us with a beautiful eight-pound baby boy name Israel Terrell Kenan and here we are fourteen years later.

Good things come to those that wait. I would like to leave with the reader that sometimes the wait can be frustrating, long, and a process but do not let the process make you but you make the process. How does one make the process? Simply, by waiting on God and knowing, believing and trusting that good things come to those that wait.

I waited patiently for the Lord; and he inclined unto me and heard my cry.
He brought me up also out of a horrible pit, out of the miry clay, and set my feet upon a rock, and established my goings. And he hath put a new song

in my mouth, even praise unto our God: many shall
see it, and fear, and shall trust in the Lord.

Psalm 40:1-3 (KJV)

On this journey, we must wait patiently for God to move and trust that God will hear and answer your cry sooner or later. Waiting on anything good in this life will allow God to move and cause you to be established in many areas of your life. So, stop singing the same old sad song and let God put a new song inside of you that will take you in this life day by day with a praise going up to our God for keeping our mind and heart during the wait. Remember, God will prove to every demon and they will see that your wait was not in vain! Keep trusting and remember good things come to those that wait!

Conclusion

 Always wait on God with any decision you have to make in life. No matter how long it may seem or take trust God and stay planted until He gives you an answer.

Prayer

Father God in the name of Jesus, give me patience while I am waiting on You to speak. Help me to stay grounded in the things of God so that my journey will go according to your will for my life.

Amen

Chapter 10

What a Man what a Man What a Mighty Mighty Good Man!

There's a Man that walks with us every step of the way on our journey of life through the good times and even the bad times. This Man is the most powerful Man not to mention the riches of them all. He can do exceeding, abundantly above anything than what you can ever think or ask. This man is full of wisdom and knowledge; in the beginning of time according to the book of Genesis He created the Heavens and the earth. On day one, God He created light, day two, firmament, day three, earth, sea and vegetation. On day four He created the sun, moon and stars. On day five, He created the birds and sea animals. On day six, He created land, animals and humans. Wow, what a Man what a Man what a mighty, mighty good Man - nobody but God himself!

This is the only man that walks with us on our journey that has multiple names, for example:

Jehovah Nissi
God is my strength

Jehovah Jireh
God will provide

Jehovah Rapha
God Heals

Jehovah Shalom
God of peace

Jehovah Raah
God way and Shepherd

Jehovah Tsidkenu
God of Righteousness

Jehovah Shanmah
God is there and ever present.

The list of name goes on and on. He is the only man that can perform miracles such as turning water into wine, healing the royal official son, healing the paralytic, Feeding well over five thousand people with two fish and five loaves of bread, He is the only man to walk on water, Heal the blind, raise the dead and the only man to die, be resurrected and set us free from all our sins past, present and future. He the only man that can complete us and make us whole and healed physically and mentally.

Scientist have tried to figure Him out and they have even tried to do what He does and failed every time because every good and perfect gift comes from above; they can never do it without Him. He created heaven and earth along with mankind, so He knows it inside out and up and down, Yes, He has let them in on some things and given them much knowledge and intelligence but can never be greater than our God. No man walking this earth can enter into the supernatural but Him because He is the supernatural. This man is God and conceived of as the supreme being, creator deity, and principal object of faith. What a Man what a Man what a mighty, mighty good Man!

By all means I had to have this Man with me on my journey. He has provided and made ways beyond my understanding, made provisions and sent His favor in my life even when I did not deserve it; that is why He is mighty. Being in this Man's presence is refreshing and life changing; that is why Satan hates when we allow God on our journey because it puts us in His presence, and he knows that God has all power in His hands! Even the demons believe and bow at His name. No matter what, He will never leave us on our journey neither forsake us. The man is so full of love and compassion and nothing can separate us from Him!

For I am persuaded, that neither death, nor life, nor angels, nor principalities, nor powers, nor things present, nor things to come, Nor height, nor depth, nor any other creature, shall be able to separate us from the love of God, which is in Christ Jesus our Lord.

Romans 8:38-39 (KJV)

It is a must that we be persuaded that God is with us and nothing, and I mean nothing, can separate us from God in this life. He is stuck to us like super glue and you must understand that walking with Him makes us unstoppable. His love is beyond any natural love that we can feel on this earth; it is supernatural. The love of God is like an anchor that is thrown out of a ship never to move. He is the captain of the ship and He must lead the way. I once heard a woman tell her story of how she had an out of body experience where she went to heaven for a few minutes. When she got there, Jesus was waiting on her with open arms. She said the love she felt just being in His presence was breathtaking.

When she looked in His eyes, it was like His love permeated through her body. She said that Jesus said to her, "Come walk with me child." As they walked together, they came to something like a pool or river of overflowing water. When they stepped in the water, she said the water healed her internally completely, and made her whole immediately. She said that Jesus walked away for a few minutes and left her. She walked up to the faucet to turn off the overflowing water, but it would not turn off. She kept trying, but the water continued to pour out and overflow. Jesus came back to her and said, "Child, what are you doing?" She replied, "I'm trying to turn off the faucet! The water is running everywhere!" Jesus said to her, "Child, you can't turn the water off. The water that you see overflowing represents My love for My people and My love for you can never be turned off. Its overflow never stops."

Wow I must say what a Man, what a Man, what a mighty, mighty good Man!

We must understand that the Man who's walking with us is not mad at us for our down falls along the way; He knew we were going to jack things up. He is not mad at us- He is madly in love with us. God is not a # 2 pencil that will erase His promises from you just because you jack things up. God's promises are yes and AMEN!

"For all the promises of God in Him *are* Yes, and in Him Amen, to the glory of God through us."
2 Corinthians 1:20 (NKJV)

His love never fails, never gives up and never runs out on us! Jesus is a mighty good Man!   I started writing this book some time ago and I stopped for many different reasons. When it was time to pick the pen back up to write I found out that I had to throw everything away. The why was simple - I needed to get in the spirit. I wanted His anointing and love to mesmerize the reader and change their lives. Even though I knew my story and what I wanted to say. I began to ask God to write this book through me and for me.

You can never find God in the natural because He is Spirit and to encounter His presence you must come up in the spirit in order to see, feel and embrace all that He has for you. I am reminded of John when he was on the island Patmos - Jesus commanded him to come up in the spirit to see some things that would take place soon, but John had to be in the spirit to see and hear these things. When we get in the spirit, God will show us what we need to see and what we need to hear. He has been walking with you and I all along the way - we just needed to get in the spirit and trust and believe that He is there walking side by side and hand and hand with us and telling us that we are His own.

God, my shepherd! I don't need a thing.
You have bedded me down in lush meadows, you find me quiet pools to drink from. True to your word, you let me catch my breath and send me in the right direction. Even when the way goes through Death Valley, I'm not afraid when you walk at my side. Your trusty shepherd's crook makes me feel secure. You serve me a six-course dinner right in front of my enemies. You revive my drooping head; my cup brims with blessing. Your beauty and love chase after me every day of my life. I'm back home in the house of God for the rest of my life.

Psalm 23 The Message (MSG)

God is true to His word. He is not like man and will not lie. I have learned that with God on this journey you will not have to want for anything; God will give you water if you are thirsty and let you take a break to get yourself together. He is just that mighty and loving.

God will always lead us in the right direction, we just have to learn to follow Him and lean not to our own understanding.

No matter what we come up against, we do not have to be afraid because our God is big, strong and mighty. Never worry about your enemies along the way because God will prepare a table for you right in front of your enemy's face. My wife preached a message once, and she made a powerful statement:

You have got to have your enemies in order to get the table! No enemies, no table!

Having this man in your life will cause you not to go on a forty-year journey. We have to trust God enough to go with His will. Trust Him and His will for our lives, and He will send blessing and miracles to our table. Yes, God will bless you right in the face of the very enemy that said you would not and that you could not and when He does we must make sure we invite them to the table and bless them like our father in Heaven would.

This Man is wrapped in beauty and love and we do not have to chase Him down. His love chases us down, captivates us and always put us back on track. Side by side He guides us on our journey. Wow! I cannot believe You chose someone like me when I have done nothing to deserve it! Lord, I feel so blessed because You gave me Your best! Your love is nothing but incredible!

What a man what a man what a mighty, mighty good man.

Conclusion

Always remember that nobody can do you like Jesus!
Put Him first and everything will work out in your favor.

Prayer

Father in the name of Jesus, help me to put you first in
my life. Give me the ability and knowledge that I need
not to continue on a forty-year journey. Make me
humble at your feet.

Amen

Connect with the Author

Steven Terrell Kenan is a native of Wallace North Carolina who now calls his home High Point, North Carolina. His greatest desire is to fulfill the purpose of God for his life and to be living proof of God's exceeding great and precious promises. Steven has a heart for God and God's people. He has availed himself in this book with his failures and victories to push and motivate people to live their best life by seeking God and putting Him first.

Steven is a man that seeks to encourage and give Godly wisdom to all men, women, boys and girls. Steven is considered to be "the soul snatcher." He desires to snatch as many souls as he can out the pit of Hell and into the plan of salvation. Steven's life is a testament that you can start out with nothing and end up with something by the power of God and staying in His plan.

Steven is the husband to Tamara Nicole Kenan, and father of one son, Israel Terrell Kenan. Steven has an Associate's degree in Biblical studies and is the Founder and Pastor of Chosen Generation Outreach Deliverance Center, Inc. where they have been in service for thirteen years in the blessed city of High Point, North Carolina.

www.ingramcontent.com/pod-product-compliance
Lightning Source LLC
Chambersburg PA
CBHW052103270326
41931CB00012B/2863